INTRODUCTION
to
REAL PRAYER

SCIENCE *of* SAINTHOOD

SCIENCE of SAINTHOOD

Nihil Obstat
The Reverend James M. Dunfee, MA, STL
Censor Librorum
March 9, 2025

Imprimatur
The Most Reverend Edward M. Lohse, JCD
Apostolic Administrator of Steubenville
March 11, 2025

The *nihil obstat* and *imprimatur* do not signify agreement with the content, opinions, or statements expressed but simply affirm that the content does not contradict faith and morals.

Video Study Written by Matthew Leonard

Workbook Written by Matthew Leonard

Workbook Edited by Curtis Mitch and Angela Von Weber-Hahnsberg

Cover Design and layout by Patty Borgman

Science Of Sainthood | ScienceOfSainthood.com

Table of Contents

Welcome to the Science of Sainthood

Welcome to *Introduction to Real Prayer*, presented by the Science of Sainthood.

Founded by evangelist Matthew Leonard, the Science of Sainthood is a leading online Catholic platform dedicated to teaching authentic Catholic spirituality. Steeped in the tradition of Saints like John of the Cross, Teresa of Avila, and Thomas Aquinas, our goal is to guide regular Catholics, step by step, down the path to nothing less than sainthood. More than education, this is *transformation*!

Introduction to Real Prayer is one of the foundational courses of the entire Science of Sainthood program. Other courses available for group study include *Catholic Mysticism & the Beautiful Life of Grace, Total Abandonment to God's Will, St. Teresa of Avila's Nine Grades of Prayer*, and *Introduction to the Psalms.* You can find out more about these studies, as well as the entire program at **ScienceOfSainthood.com**.

Study Materials

Introduction to Real Prayer can be done by an individual or in a group. There are four possible components of this study:

• The *Introduction to Real Prayer* participant workbook

• A leader guide

• The video lessons (There are nine lessons in this series.)

• *Prayer Works: Getting a Grip on Catholic Spirituality* by Matthew Leonard

All materials for this and other studies can be purchased at **ScienceOfSainthood.com**.

How to Use This Workbook

Each lesson in this study contains the following sections:

• Short Introduction

• Review of the Previous Lesson

• Lesson Video

• Space to Take Notes on the Video Lesson

• A Passage from a Saint

• A Guided Audio Meditation & Scripture Passage

• A Written Meditation for Further Reflection

• Review & Discussion Questions

• Suggested Further Reading

• Prayer Journal

While the format is essentially self-explanatory, the following information is intended to help you get the most out of this workbook.

🔊 Guided Audio Meditation with Scripture

As noted above, in addition to the video, each lesson has an accompanying guided audio meditation that matches the scripture passage in the workbook. It is intended to help you begin practicing simple meditative prayer right away. If you have access to the series online, you will find the audio meditation online right after each video lesson. **(If you are part of a group study and want to purchase access to the videos and audio meditations, you can do so at a very large discount on the next page.)**

If you would like to journal at any time, there is space provided in the Prayer Journal section at the end of the lesson.

Review & Discussion Questions

We have provided Review and Discussion Questions to help individuals and groups with their recollection of the material and spur group discussion. Answers to the Review Questions are located in the Course Study Materials folder found with the video lessons online. (The folder is located before Lesson One.)

▌ Further Reading

At the end of every lesson there is a section titled "Further Reading" and shows where you can go to explore the topic of the lesson more deeply. This video series is based on (and follows the format of) Matthew Leonard's *Prayer Works: Getting a Grip on Catholic Spirituality*. Copies can be purchased at ScienceOfSainthood.com or by scanning the QR Code on the next page.

Finally, don't forget this study is just one of many within the Science of Sainthood. To see more group and individual courses or learn about full access to all the Science of Sainthood studies, visit **ScienceOfSainthood.com**!

Are you in a Group Study But Want to Watch on Your Own, Too?

Enjoy the course on your own time with a **huge discount** on a One Year rental of *Introduction to Real Prayer*.

And don't forget to get a copy of the book this series is based on!

Access all the lessons on your own!

Savor this course at home with a full year of access to every lesson on your computer and mobile devices at a huge discount!

Get the book this series is based on!

Go deeper into this great series with a copy of Matthew's book *Prayer Works: Getting a Grip on Catholic Spirituality*.

"Best book on prayer I have ever read!!"

GET THEM BOTH!

Scan the QR Code with your Phone's Camera & Tap the Link!

LESSON ONE

Why Pray?

Lesson Introduction

There's no way around the fact that prayer is one of the most important topics that we need to understand and engage in. It is the manner through which God determined that we further our relationship and communicate with him. If we're not praying, we're not talking to the Person who not only created us, but loves us more than we can fathom.

 **NOW BEGIN THE VIDEO**

Notes

What the Saints Say

"Prayer is the place of refuge for every worry, a foundation for cheerfulness, a source of constant happiness, a protection against sadness."

ST. JOHN CHRYSOSTOM — *4th Century Archbishop of Constantinople & Doctor of the Church*

🔊 Play Guided Audio Meditation

Note: *If you have access to the course online you'll find the guided audio meditation under Lesson One. If you are part of a group, your leader will play the meditation for you.*

"Rejoice in the Lord always; again I will say, Rejoice. Let all men know your forbearance. The Lord is at hand.

Have no anxiety about anything, but in everything by prayer and supplication with thanksgiving let your requests be made known to God. And the peace of God, which passes all understanding, will keep your hearts and your minds in Christ Jesus."

PHILIPPIANS 4:4–7

Further Reflection

Anxiety is a plague. Given the difficulties of life, it's difficult for many of us to not be anxious about so many things. But we don't have to be. What many people never discover is that prayer is one of the surest ways to alleviate anxiety. In fact, you could say that anxiety and prayer shouldn't co-exist—at least in a perfect world.

Why? Because prayer is our relationship with God. It is a continuous movement into the depths of divine life. And the more we move into union with God, the more we rest in the fact that our identity is that of a child of God. So why should we be anxious? After all, the God of the universe is in love with us! He wants to pour himself out upon us! He wants to give us the power and protection to weather any and all storms of life.

Seek the Lord in prayer and watch your anxiety begin to melt away like snow on a warm, Spring day. As Matthew 6:31–33 declares, "Do not be anxious, saying, 'What shall we eat?' or 'What shall we drink?' or 'What shall we wear?' For the Gentiles seek all these things; and your heavenly Father knows that you need them all. But seek first his kingdom and his righteousness, and all these things shall be yours as well."

Review Questions

1. At its core, what is prayer a movement of?

2. Why are we made to pray?

3. What does prayer take our eyes off of and turn our gaze toward?

4. According to the *Catechism of the Catholic Church*, is it enough to have the will to pray? Why?

Discussion Questions

1. Have you ever thought about the fact that you are made to pray? Does that give you a different perspective on why you need to have a life of prayer?

2. Did any of the definitions of prayer given by the saints or the *Catechism* strike you? If someone asked you how to define prayer, what would you say?

3. What is it that you hope to gain through this study on prayer? Is there anything in particular you're wondering about?

4. What does your prayer life look like right now? How often do you set time aside for God?

5. If you were to be totally honest with yourself, do you feel fulfilled in life? If not, what do you think you're lacking? Does it make sense that a deeper life of prayer would lead to deeper contentment?

📖 Further Reading

Chapter 1 of *Prayer Works: Getting a Grip on Catholic Spirituality* by Matthew Leonard

Prayer Journal

LESSON TWO

Beginning to Really Pray

What We Covered in Our Last Lesson

Prayer is perhaps the single most important topic you'll ever study. Along with the sacraments, it's a primary avenue by which we enter into a relationship with God. As such, it's the secret to earthly happiness, peace, and fulfillment. It's a key to attaining heaven.

(If you're interested in reading more on prayer, get a copy of *Prayer Works: Getting a Grip on Catholic Spirituality*. It provides a very easy to read, in-depth guide to real prayer and serves as a companion to this course. You can find it along with Matthew's other books and courses at www.ScienceOfSainthood.com.)

An unfortunate but common misconception about prayer is that it consists mostly of the boring, mindless repetition of certain words. That couldn't be further from the truth. Real prayer is an outpouring of our hearts to God—deep, authentic communication with the Person who loves us more than anyone else. God literally made us for this communication; he made us to have a genuine relationship with him and become a part of his family in a very real, personal way.

The *Catechism of the Catholic Church* says that "prayer is the encounter of God's thirst with ours" (CCC 2560). God thirsts for you. His greatest desire is to draw you into a union of love that is beyond anything you can possibly imagine. And it all revolves around your life of prayer.

In this study, we're going to examine the basics of what prayer is and how to do it, so that we can enter into that real, personal relationship with God. We will explore the 3 major types of prayer to which *all* Catholics (not just priests or religious) are called—vocal, meditative, and contemplative prayer. We'll also address common issues like distraction, dryness, and spiritual darkness, discussing what they are, why they happen, and how to deal with them. Ultimately, our goal in this study of prayer is to ignite a raging inferno of love for God and a deep desire to be radically transformed.

The first question we should ask is, "What is prayer?". Paragraph 2650 of the *Catechism* says, "Prayer cannot be reduced to the spontaneous outpouring of interior impulse: in order to pray, one must have the will to pray. Nor is it enough to know what the Scriptures reveal about prayer: one must also learn how to pray."

Prayer is not something that just happens automatically. There's an art to prayer that the Church tells us we need to learn—and just like anything else, the more you practice it, the better you get. And realize that just knowing about prayer isn't enough; you have to actually engage in it.

Many saints offer helpful definitions of prayer. "For me," says St. Thérèse of Lisieux, "prayer is a surge of the heart; it is a simple look turned toward heaven, it is a cry of recognition and of love, embracing both trial and joy" (CCC 2558). Similarly, the eighth century Church Father St. John Damascene says, "Prayer is the raising of one's mind and heart to God or the requesting of good things from God" (CCC 2559).

St. Teresa of Ávila, the famous 16th century Spanish mystic and Doctor of Prayer, says "prayer in my opinion is nothing else than an intimate sharing between friends; it means taking time frequently to be alone with Him who we know loves us."[1]

These quotes show us that at its core, prayer is a movement of love. It's the raising of our hearts toward God. To put it another way, prayer comes from that place deep inside ourselves to which we withdraw—our interior life—that conversation that takes place inside when we're alone with ourselves. Prayer is so important because all too often those little conversations in our head revolve around one thing—us. But when the grace of prayer begins acting on our lives, that interior conversation moves from something that is self-centered, to something God-centered. It takes our eyes off of ourselves and puts them on God.

And this God-centered relationship is what every person ever created actually wants, even if they don't realize it. It's hard-coded into our DNA because we were made for union with God. That's why people with no interior life—no life of prayer—are so unfulfilled and ultimately unhappy. They keep trying to fill their emptiness with things that will never satisfy. And they remain unsatisfied because humans are made for more than anything this world can offer. We're made for relationship with the Divine Other who created us. That's why prayer is so vitally important. It is our communication with God. It is that filling up with God that heals our lonely, dissatisfied souls.

Prayer not only *acknowledges* God's presence, through it we move *toward* Him. We look into his eyes. And what do we see? We see a God who loves us more than we can possibly imagine. "God is love," says 1 John 4:8, and he wants to pour that love into us in a way that essentially defies description. The Lord longs for us with a depth of desire that we can't even fathom. The whole reason he created us was because of his overflowing love and his desire to draw us into that breathtaking, all-encompassing love.

---

[1] *Teresa of Avila: The Book of Her Life,* Chapter 8

In light of this incredible reality, it's a mistake to view prayer as something we have to do. Rather than something we do for God, prayer is something he does for us. It's a gift that he gives us, a channel through which we can enter into union with Him. It's the path to a peace and fulfillment unlike anything else.

Lesson Introduction

Now that we've discussed why we should pray and have laid some foundation, we're going to zero in on the most common form of prayer, particularly for beginners—petition. In addition to discussing why it's so necessary (and even good), we'll answer some common questions like:

1. If God already knows what we're going to ask, why should we pray?

&

2. What kinds of things should we be praying for?

 **NOW BEGIN THE VIDEO**

Notes

What the Saints Say

"We must speak to God as a friend speaks to his friend... now asking some favor, now acknowledging our faults, and communicating to Him all that concerns us, our thoughts, our fears, our projects, our desires, and in all things seeking His counsel."

ST. IGNATIUS OF LOYOLA—*16th Century Founder of the Society of Jesus (Jesuits) & author of the famous Spiritual Exercises*

Play Guided Audio Meditation

"Ask, and it will be given you; seek, and you will find; knock, and it will be opened to you. For every one who asks receives, and he who seeks finds, and to him who knocks it will be opened.

Or what man of you, if his son asks him for bread, will give him a stone? Or if he asks for a fish, will give him a serpent?

If you then, who are evil, know how to give good gifts to your children, how much more will your Father who is in heaven give good things to those who ask him!"

MATTHEW 7:7–11

Further Reflection

God is your Father... Let that sink in.

The God who created the universe and holds your very being in existence is your Daddy. It's almost too ludicrous to say, let alone wrap your mind around. But that's why prayer is so ridiculously important. It's the way we communicate with Our perfect Father in heaven, the Maker of everything.

And never forget that he is longing to pour out upon you undreamed of spiritual riches. In fact, he's begging you to ask them of Him. There is nothing he loves more than giving his children the greatest gifts they could ever receive!

That said, he's not going to force you. He's not that kind of Father. He's waiting patiently at the door of your heart. You have to open it. You have to invite him in. Don't wait. Seek him in prayer.

Review Questions

1. What is the goal of our lives?

2. Why is it that human beings (unlike the rest of creation) can even aspire to pray to the God of the universe?

3. What is the relationship between prayer and the grace of the sacraments? What does prayer do?

4. If we reject prayer who are we actually rejecting?

5. What is the primary form of prayer for most beginners and why is it good?

6. Why should we pray if God already knows what we're going to ask for?

Discussion Questions

1. Matthew 6:33 says, "Seek first his kingdom and his righteousness, and all these things shall be yours as well." What do you think about the idea that our first goal should be to prioritize praying for things that will lead us to heaven? Does that make sense to you? Why or why not?

2. Sometimes when people repeatedly ask us for things, we can get annoyed. That's not the case with our perfect Father in heaven. Have you ever meditated on the fact that God likes it when we ask him for good things? Does that understanding affect your desire to turn to him on a regular basis?

3. Scripture is very clear that the Lord knows exactly what you need and promises to answer your petitions in the manner that is best for you. (Philippians 4:6–7; 1 John 5:14; Luke 11:9–13) Do you trust that God always hears you and is going to answer your prayers in the best manner for you? Can you think of an example of when this happened?

4. Most of us have had the experience of being rejected by others. From failed relationships to cancelled appointments and everything in-between, the message often conveyed is "there is something more important that requires my time."

And while many times there are legitimate reasons for these situations, many of them cause us hurt and pain. And while God doesn't feel "pain" so to speak, have you ever considered the fact that a rejection of prayer is essentially a rejection of him? Does that alter your view of prayer? If so, how?

Further Reading

Chapter 2 of *Prayer Works: Getting a Grip on Catholic Spirituality* by Matthew Leonard

Prayer Journal

LESSON THREE

The Map to God

What We Covered in Our Last Lesson

Prayer is a non-negotiable. There is nothing that can replace it. Without it, our spiritual life will suffocate and die. And if we've got no spiritual life, we've got no communication with God.

If you don't make prayer an absolute priority, it will be the first thing thrown off your "to-do" list when things get busy. And when we reject our time of prayer, we're essentially rejecting relationship and communication with God. Just like any human relationship needs care and attention to grow, so too does our relationship with our Heavenly Father—the most important relationship in our lives!

Don't forget that the entire point of the Catholic life is to conform ourselves to Christ. It's not about just becoming his friend—we're supposed to become holy in and through Him. As St. Peter says in 1 Peter 1:15–16, "As he who called you is holy, be holy yourselves in all your conduct; since it is written, 'You shall be holy, for I am holy.'"

So the goal is for us to live holy lives in deep union with him, to live in real relationship with him. Prayer is essential to that relationship. But because Original Sin disrupted our communication with God, we need to learn how to converse well with him again. We need to learn how to pray.

But why is it that human beings can even dream of and aspire to be in relationship with the God of the universe? The answer is found in the beginning of the Bible. In Genesis 1:26, God said, "Let us make man in our image, after our likeness." But while they retained his image, when Adam and Eve sinned, there is a sense in which they lost their likeness to God. They destroyed their relationship with him by seeking to elevate themselves and selfishly grasping the divine life that God was offering. In other words, they acted the complete opposite of how the New Adam, Jesus Christ acted when he emptied and lowered himself for our sake. And because Adam and Eve lost their likeness to God, you could say the whole Catholic life is about getting that likeness back. How do we do that?

"Prayer," says the *Catechism*, "restores man to God's likeness and enables him to share in the power of God's love" (CCC 2572). That's the reason prayer is so vital. It's a big part of how the wound of Original Sin is healed and we're restored to God's family, how we become like the Most Holy Trinity.

Of course, prayer doesn't exist in a vacuum. It's wedded to the sacraments. But without prayer, the grace of the sacraments doesn't flow. Prayer clears the path so that God's grace can transform us into the likeness of Jesus Christ.

And we have to understand what an incredible gift prayer is! Certainly, before the time of Jesus, people could interact with God on friendly terms. Exodus 33:11 says Moses used to speak "face to face" with God, "as a man speaks to his friend." But Christ brought the relationship to a whole new level. As the Son of God, he cries out to the Father and actually calls him "Abba, Father" (Mark 14:36). And through him, we can do the same. St. Paul declares that we have received a "spirit of sonship," so that "when we cry 'Abba!' Father! it is the Spirit himself bearing witness with our spirit that we are children of God" (Romans 8:15–16). This is our new reality in the New Covenant of Jesus Christ. We can pray at a whole new level!

Of course, when someone mentions prayer, most people think of one particular kind of prayer—petition. This is when we make requests of God for things that we want or need. Petitionary prayer is a good thing. Why?

Because in asking God for things, we're recognizing that he is the source of everything. Petitionary prayer recognizes that God is Creator and we are creature, that God is Father and we are children, that God is the Giver and we are the receiver of his gifts. In fact, like any good Father, God expects us to ask him for things. As St. Paul says in Philippians 4:6, "Have no anxiety about anything, but in everything by prayer and supplication with thanksgiving let your requests be made known to God."

It's pretty incredible. All we have to do to reach out to the God of the universe is to start talking. And it's more powerful than we realize. The *Roman Catechism* declares that "prayer is the indispensable instrument given us by God in order to obtain what we desire: there are things, in fact, impossible to obtain without the aid of prayer."

So what should we be praying for? All things being equal, we should prioritize asking for things that will lead us to heaven. That's the main goal. Our ultimate happiness lies in God. So our first priority should be to pray for supernatural graces to help us move closer to him. Then we move on to our material needs.

We pray for our needs in this order because it's the order given to us by Christ himself. In Matthew 6:33, he says, "Seek first his kingdom and his righteousness, and all these things shall be yours as well." Jesus is basically saying that if we put God first, he'll take care of the rest. Yes, it's very likely that we will undergo even serious hardship at some point since we live in a fallen world. But in the end, our perfect Father in heaven will make sure it all works to our good. That's exactly what is promised in Romans 8:28. "We know that in everything God works for good with those who love him, who are called according to his purpose."

Lesson Introduction

The spiritual life isn't supposed to be static. Our job is not to simply tread spiritual water so that when we die (or Jesus returns) we'll be found in a state of grace. We're supposed to make real progress. We're supposed to grow.

And while the vast majority of Catholics have never heard of them, Catholic doctrine and tradition teach that there are three different stages of growth in the spiritual life that each of us will go through. These stages provide us with an invaluable map to God, letting us know both where we are and what's coming our way.

 **NOW BEGIN THE VIDEO**

Notes

What the Saints Say

"If a thick black cloth be placed over a crystal in the sunshine, however, it is clear that, although the sun may be shining upon it, its brightness will have no effect upon the crystal."

ST. TERESA OF ÁVILA—*16th Century Spanish Mystic & the Doctor of Prayer*

🔊 Play Guided Audio Meditation

"See what love the Father has given us, that we should be called children of God; and so we are. The reason why the world does not know us is that it did not know him.

Beloved, we are God's children now; it does not yet appear what we shall be, but we know that when he appears we shall be like him, for we shall see him as he is.

And every one who thus hopes in him purifies himself as he is pure."

1 JOHN 3:1–3

Further Reflection

When you ponder on how we're supposed to grow up in the spiritual life, a question sometimes arises. Namely, how do we reconcile our need to grow up and mature in the faith with Jesus' statement that "Unless you turn and become like children, you will never enter the kingdom of heaven" (Matthew 18:3)?

In fact, the entire idea behind the famous "Little Way"— the spirituality of St. Thérèse of Lisieux—is based on the notion that we are to remain little and childlike.

So which is it? Are we supposed to stay children or become mature adults? The answer is that they're both the same thing. How? Well, the more we grow up in the spiritual life, the more we understand our identity as children.

You see, when Christ says we must become like a child, he doesn't mean we remain immature little kids who don't know how to behave or act. He means that we understand who we are in relation to God the Father. He means we need to learn to fully trust and give ourselves over to a Father who will take care of all our needs and bless us.

And the more we mature and make progress in the spiritual life, the more deeply we do just that—become a child who abandons themselves completely into God's hands.

Of course, prayer is a major part of this trust and growth because the more we pray, the more it gradually sinks in that our Father is literally the King of the universe who loves us more than we can imagine. And if he's the King of everything, why wouldn't we want to more fully trust him?

Review Questions

1. What are the 3 stages of the spiritual life and what is their role?

2. What is the Purgative Way?

3. How do we get into the Purgative Way to begin with?

4. What does St. Teresa of Ávila emphasize as a terrible danger in the early stages of the spiritual life?

5. How do we make war on sin and grow in the Purgative Way?

6. What sensation will we experience in our prayer life as we transition from the Purgative Way to the Illuminative way?

7. What do we focus more upon once we enter into the Illuminative way?

8. What do we become filled with in the Unitive way?

Discussion Questions

1. Before this lesson had you ever heard of the three stages of the spiritual life? Does it make sense to you that we grow up in the spiritual life in a manner similar to growing up in the natural life?

2. Can you think of a time in your life, growing up, when you remember making a real leap in maturity? Now think of your progress in the spiritual life. Have you seen that same kind of "growth spurt" in your spiritual life? If so, what was the cause of that growth? If not, why do you think it hasn't happened?

3. Have you ever had a spiritual director, mentor, or friend who has accompanied you in your spiritual life? If so, what was your experience like? Did they help you grow in the interior life? Why or why not? If you've never had someone accompany you as a spiritual friend or mentor, have you ever considered finding one?

4. Why do you think that prayer is one of the major keys to making progress in the Purgative Way? In light of what we've been studying, what would need to change about your personal prayer life in order to truly start working your way through this stage?

5. Matthew will discuss the topic of dryness in more detail later in the study, but have you already experienced it in prayer? If so, what was that like, and how did you get through it? If you're still in it, what have you learned so far in this study that would help you deal with it? Is there anything you're struggling with in prayer right now? What areas of prayer do you need help in?

Optional Prayer Exercise

Many people spend a very long time in the Purgative Way. Without naming them out loud, take a few moments and think of any larger sins or struggles that may be keeping you from making progress. Once they come to mind, say a quiet prayer asking the Lord for help to combat them.

Further Reading

Chapters 3–4 of *Prayer Works: Getting a Grip on Catholic Spirituality* by Matthew Leonard

Prayer Journal

LESSON FOUR

The Surprising Power of Vocal Prayer

What We Covered in Our Last Lesson

Prayer isn't something that just comes naturally and requires no effort. Nor is it random or haphazard. It follows a particular path. In fact, the entire spiritual life follows a particular path. We're all headed toward a particular destination: heaven. And that means there must be a particular path. That path is known as the three stages of the spiritual life and it is directly related to the life of prayer.

Many Catholics have never heard of these three stages. But if you went back into the early centuries of the Church you'd find direct teaching about them, beginning in the third century writings of Origen. In the fourth and fifth centuries they're found in the teachings of Evagrius Ponticus, St. Gregory of Nyssa, and Dionysius the Areopagite.

The three stages were also beautifully taught in the 16th and 17th centuries by Doctors of the Church like Saints John of the Cross, Teresa of Ávila, and Francis de Sales, among others. And they weren't pulling them out of thin air. You'll find allusions to the stages in Sacred Scripture, particularly in the writings of St. Paul (cf. 1 Corinthians 9:26–27; Philippians 3; 2 Cor. 12).

The traditional names of these three stages are the Purgative, Illuminative, and Unitive ways. The first stage, or the Purgative Way, is a kind of initial cleansing process. After our initial conversion, our lives need to be purged of sin, particularly mortal sin. And that cleansing and purging continues until we enter into the Illuminative Way—or second stage—where we are "illuminated" by the light and love of God.

In this second stage we become more focused on pulling up the deeper weeds of sin, growing in serious virtue, and radically deepening our prayer life. And this more intense focus upon prayer and virtue continues until we are eventually unified with God in the final stage of spiritual growth—the Unitive Way. The Unitive Way is the pinnacle of the spiritual life on earth. It's where our lives are full to the brim with the Holy Spirit and we're completely consumed with God.

St. Thomas Aquinas describes the three stages as a movement from spiritual infancy, into spiritual adolescence, and finally spiritual adulthood. Just as we grow up in the natural life, we grow up in the spiritual life. But the three stages are not mutually exclusive. As you mature in the spiritual life, they can overlap and intermingle. That said, one of them will predominate depending upon your progress.

The three stages are important because they tell us where we are in the spiritual life and what we can look forward to as we make progress. But the point of learning the three stages isn't to navel gaze. Some people get so caught up in trying to figure out exactly where they are that they lose sight of the fact that they're supposed to be making progress.

We also have to realize that, more often than not, we're not the best judge of our own spiritual life. Sin blinds us to our own faults, so having a good spiritual director, mentor, or solid spiritual friendships can be extremely helpful. Even so, it's still crucial to have an understanding of the stages ourselves, because they tell us where we're going and what to expect so we can avoid pitfalls as we travel toward our end.

When we talk about people in the three stages, we're talking about those who are baptized and living the life of grace. Once you lose your baptismal innocence through sin, the sacrament of Confession is your doorway back in. If you're not joined to Christ, you're not even in the Purgative Way.

PURGATIVE WAY

Once we become spiritually aware, we begin to realize that we've got some major sins and bad habits that need to be dealt with. We're still extremely weak in this first stage and the Devil does everything he can to throw us back into spiritual darkness. But as long as we persevere and make war on our sinful habits, we get stronger and begin to make spiritual progress. This spiritual war is waged by getting to the sacraments, as well as by regular prayer, particularly meditation. You cannot separate prayer and spiritual growth.

Typically, once you learn to quiet yourself interiorly and are able to focus your prayers, these early days of prayer are a very sweet time of communing with the Lord. That said, after a while, things are going to change, and you have to know what's coming your way in the life of prayer or you will get frustrated and stop. In particular, this "change" manifests itself as dryness in prayer. Whereas you really felt the presence of God early on, now you begin to lose that sensation and ease of communion. This happens because God is beginning to work more deeply on you. He's teaching you to grow up and seek him for who he is instead of what you feel or what good things you can receive from him.

In fact, this dryness plays an important role in the three stages. It's part of the gradual transition between the first and second stages, the Purgative and Illuminative Ways. Since it is a natural part of the process, don't be discouraged when it happens.

Lesson Introduction

While there are three different universal types of prayer, the most common is vocal prayer. And while there's a sense in which it's the "bottom rung," it's something we never leave behind as we progress up the divine ladder. As the *Catechism of the Catholic Church* declares, it "is an essential element of the Christian life" (CCC 2701).

Let's find out why.

 **NOW BEGIN THE VIDEO**

Notes

_____

_____

_____

_____

_____

_____

_____

_____

_____

_____

What the Saints Say

"Vocal prayer ... must be accompanied by reflection. A prayer in which a person is not aware of Whom he is speaking to, what he is asking, who it is who is asking and of Whom, I don't call prayer—however much the lips may move."

ST. TERESA OF ÁVILA—*16th Century Spanish Mystic & the Doctor of Prayer*

⏯ Play Guided Audio Meditation

"Therefore take the whole armor of God, that you may be able to withstand in the evil day, and having done all, to stand.

Stand therefore, having girded your loins with truth, and having put on the breastplate of righteousness, and having shod your feet with the equipment of the gospel of peace; above all taking the shield of faith, with which you can quench all the flaming darts of the evil one. And take the helmet of salvation, and the sword of the Spirit, which is the word of God.

Pray at all times in the Spirit, with all prayer and supplication. To that end keep alert with all perseverance, making supplication for all the saints."

EPHESIANS 6:13–18

Further Reflection

Isn't it interesting where St. Paul places the admonition to "pray at all times" in the Ephesians 6 passage? It's not where you'd necessarily expect it, like in a discussion of the liturgy or the sacraments (though prayer is certainly a part of both). Instead, he puts it in the context of war...spiritual war.

Paul is telling us that arming ourselves for battle with the Evil One demands prayer. Not just a little, but at all times. Certainly this takes time to develop, but we need to start working on it now. We must call God to mind as often as possible during the day. After all, the Devil is relentless. And we must match the ferocity of his desire to kill with an iron clad defense and powerful counter-attack. Truth, righteousness, peace, faith, and salvation are dependent upon prayer.

We must be constant. We must persevere. Souls—starting with our own—depend upon it.

Review Questions

1. What are the different forms of prayer listed in the *Catechism*?

2. Why are there so many different forms of prayer?

3. What does it mean to "bless" God?

4. Does anyone besides God deserve adoration and worship?

5. What kind of prayer asks God for things and why is it necessary?

6. What is intercessory prayer?

7. While all of them play a role, what form of prayer is most central to the Mass?

8. Why is vocal prayer so important and powerful?

Discussion Questions

1. Which forms of prayer do you typically make use of the most in your prayer life? After studying all the different types in this lesson, are there any you would like to practice more?

2. Think of a time in your life when you went through hardship or trial. Did you feel able to give thanks to God even in the midst of it? If yes, is there something in particular that helped you to do that? If not, what kept you from being able to do so? Was there something in this lesson that might help you approach future trials in a way that allows you to thank God through it all?

3. When talking to God, do you typically pray to the Father, Son, or Holy Spirit? Do you have a devotion to Our Lady or turn to a particular saint in time of need?

4. St. John Chrysostom said, "Whether or not our prayer is heard depends not on the number of words, but on the fervor of our souls" (CCC 2700). Jesus said, "In praying do not heap up empty phrases as the Gentiles do; for they think that they will be heard for their many words" (Matthew 6:7).

Do these quotes describe your own life of prayer? Have you ever fallen into the habit of heaping up words because you think that unless you say it, God won't understand or act? What might this reveal about your view of God?

5. Have you ever experienced the power of vocal prayer in a special way? Maybe you got chills hearing a crowd reciting the rosary together, or felt great emotion personally expressing yourself to God out loud? Was there something in particular you think made it so moving?

Further Reading

Chapters 5–6 of *Prayer Works: Getting a Grip on Catholic Spirituality* by Matthew Leonard

Prayer Journal

LESSON FIVE

Moving into Meditative Prayer

What We Covered in Our Last Lesson

Because the way we pray changes depending upon the situation we're in, there are several different forms of prayer. The *Catechism* lists them as: blessing and adoration, petition, intercession, thanksgiving, and praise.

At first blush, it might seem odd that we bless God, but we can do so because he provides the initial blessing. In other words, he blesses us and so we bless him. An example would be the Divine Praises that we often recite during eucharistic adoration.

"Blessed be God."

"Blessed be his holy Name."

"Blessed be Jesus Christ, true God and true Man," and so on.

As the *Catechism* says, "The prayer of blessing is man's response to God's gifts: because God blesses, the human heart can in return bless the One who is the source of every blessing" (CCC 2626).

The *Catechism* pairs adoration with blessing because adoration "exalts the greatness of the Lord who made us" (CCC 2628, Cf. Ps 95:1–6). It puts us in a position to receive God's blessing in the first place so we can in turn bless him.

Related to this is the fact that oftentimes Catholics are accused by our Protestant brethren of worshipping the Virgin Mary or other saints. That is simply false. The Church is crystal clear that God alone is worthy of adoration. We give what's called *latria*—adoration—to God alone. The opposite of *latria* is *idolatria*, or idolatry. We give a special kind of veneration to Mary called *hyper-dulia*, and we give *dulia* to the rest of the saints. We honor and venerate them, but we don't worship them.

While blessing and adoration are listed first in the *Catechism*, the first kind of prayer most people think of is petition. That's because it seems we're always asking God for something. This isn't a bad thing because the truth is that we have to ask God for things. Petitionary prayer puts us in the proper role of children asking our Father for sustenance and help.

Another form of prayer is intercession, which is done on behalf of another person in need.

Intercessory prayer is powerful because it "leads us to pray as Jesus did," says the *Catechism* (CCC 2634). It helps us because we're acting like Christ, and it helps the other person for whom we're praying.

If we've matured enough to be grateful for undeserved gifts, thanksgiving, a fourth kind of vocal prayer, should be one of our most natural forms. It's a good idea to make prayers of thanksgiving part of your opening dialogue with God whenever you enter into prayer. St. Paul starts and ends most of his letters with thanksgiving. In 1 Thessalonians 5:18, for example, he encourages us to "give thanks in all circumstances; for this is the will of God in Christ Jesus for you."

This isn't always easy, particularly when experiencing hardships. But learning to thank God in every circumstance is a sure and powerful sign of spiritual growth.

The biggest act of thanksgiving in our life is the Mass. The greatest thing God gives us in this life is himself in the Eucharist. The *Catechism* says that every Eucharistic liturgy is a "sacrifice of thanksgiving to the Father" (CCC 1360). *Eucharistia*, the Greek word from which we get "*Eucharist*," literally means "thanksgiving."

The final form of prayer in the *Catechism* is praise. Praising God gives him glory simply for who he is. Progress in prayer always entails the prayer of praise. The *Catechism* says it "embraces the other forms of prayer and carries them toward" God (CCC 2639).

These forms of prayer don't exist in a vacuum. They operate within the framework of the three *universal* modes or expressions of prayer which are known as vocal, meditative, and contemplative prayer. These three universal modes form a kind of progression or ladder in the life of prayer as we move into deeper communion with God. And the first step on the ladder, so to speak, is vocal prayer.

Most of us know a lot of vocal prayers, such as the Our Father and Hail Mary. Vocal prayer is extremely important for us as human beings because we are a union of body and soul. The *Catechism* says that as embodied persons, "we experience the need to translate our feelings externally" (CCC 2702). For example, we kneel, fold our hands, and bow our heads to pray. Why? Because we're expressing interior reverence exteriorly through our body.

Vocal prayer works the same way. It's an external "voicing" of our interior life. Even if you progress all the way into the highest of heights in the spiritual life, you don't leave vocal prayer behind. The *Catechism* says it remains "an essential element of the Christian life" (CCC 2701). Also, don't forget that words are incredibly powerful. While not as powerful as the words of God, our words are certainly powerful enough to affect many things.

Finally, vocal prayer is important because our prayer lives aren't just personal. There is real power when the family of God is praying together, especially in the liturgy.

Of course, just saying words isn't prayer. As St. John Chrysostom said, "Whether or not our prayer is heard depends not on the number of words, but on the fervor of our souls" (CCC 2700). In other words, we have to focus on what we're saying.

While vocal prayer is its own category of prayer, you can't totally separate it from meditation and contemplation. That's because though it's an exterior prayer, it's expressing an interior reality. And the more your words are focused upon what's going on inside of you, the more meditative or even contemplative your vocal prayers can become. The *Catechism* even says when we're really focused on what we're saying, "vocal prayer becomes an initial form of contemplative prayer" (CCC 2704). In other words, prayer is all connected because it's all communicating and relating to God. It's all part of the same relationship.

Lesson Introduction

While vocal prayer remains essential to the spiritual life no matter how far up the divine ladder you climb, there are two more universal expressions of prayer that are vitally important—meditation and contemplation.

And while we'll learn in a coming lesson that there's a sense in which contemplative prayer is a complete and utter gift of God, meditation is something we can (and should) be doing regularly now. In fact, if more Catholics had a real life of meditative prayer, this world would be a very different place.

That said, there's a lot of confusion about exactly what meditation is and how to do it. This lesson is about dispelling that confusion.

 **NOW BEGIN THE VIDEO**

Notes

What the Saints Say

"He who does not make mental prayer does not even know his defects, and therefore, as St. Bernard says, he does not abhor them. He does not even know the dangers to which his eternal salvation is exposed, and, therefore, he does not even think of avoiding them.

But he who applies himself to meditation instantly sees his faults, and the dangers of perdition, and, seeing them, he will reflect on the remedies for them."

ST. ALPHONSUS LIGOURI—*18th Century Bishop & Doctor of the Church*

🔊 Play Guided Audio Meditation

"My soul is feasted as with marrow and fat,

and my mouth praises thee with joyful lips,

when I think of thee upon my bed,

and meditate on thee in the watches of the night;

for thou hast been my help,

and in the shadow of thy wings I sing for joy.

My soul clings to thee;

thy right hand upholds me."

PSALM 63:5–8

Further Reflection

We think about things that are important to us.

How often have we been lost in thought about the beloved person who stole our heart? How much time have we spent deliberating over issues at work or events on the homefront?

Meditating upon something allows it to seep into your being. It begins to consume you. You sear it into your memory. That's why we need to meditate on God. We need to focus upon him and allow him to soak into the marrow of our spiritual bones so as to become one with us.

As the Book of Proverbs says, "Be attentive to my words; incline your ear to my sayings. Let them not escape from your sight; keep them within your heart. For they are life to him who finds them, and healing to all his flesh" (4:20–22). Scripture is telling us that we need to open ourselves to the torrent of divine love that can only be accessed through meditative prayer. It's one of the most important things in the spiritual life... by far. There is no substitute for it. It is something we *must* practice.

As St. Teresa of Ávila writes in *The Way of Perfection*, "Meditation is the basis for acquiring all the virtues, and to undertake it is a matter of life and death for all Christians."

Review Questions

1. What is the simple definition of meditation?

2. Why are we not trying to empty our minds in Catholic meditative prayer?

3. Why do we use physical things to help us talk to God?

4. How do you set the exterior stage for meditative prayer?

5. What are some practical ways to calm yourself down interiorly for meditation?

6. What are the steps to meditation?

Discussion Questions

1. Do you practice meditation on a regular basis? If not, why? If so, is the way you learned to meditate the same or similar to how it is described in the lesson? What's your favorite "input" to use for meditation?

2. In the lesson, Matthew quoted St. Teresa of Ávila who said, "If you do not practice mental prayer, you do not need any devil to throw you into hell, you throw yourself in there of your own accord." How does that statement strike you?

3. Everyone struggles in prayer at some point. What do you find to be the most difficult aspect of meditation or prayer in general? Have you had success in overcoming it? If not, what steps might help you to do so?

4. Were you aware of the differences between Catholic meditative prayer and that of non-Catholic spiritualities? Have you ever practiced non-Catholic meditation? Does it make sense that God wants to deepen our identity as his children by filling us up and making us like him through meditation, as opposed to some kind of emptying our minds or "harmonizing us" somehow with nature?

5. If you could make an ideal plan for daily prayer, what would it look like? Where and when would you meditate? What physical input would you use? How can you make this ideal plan a reality? If you can't do all of it right away, what can you begin doing now?

Further Reading

Chapter 7 of *Prayer Works: Getting a Grip on Catholic Spirituality* by Matthew Leonard

Prayer Journal

LESSON SIX

Spiritual Consolations & Dealing with Dryness

What We Covered in Our Last Lesson

The second type or universal expression of prayer is meditation, or mental prayer. Meditation is attentive reflection on God helped by some kind of physical input. It's a quiet, interior conversation between you and God using a physical tool like a book, art, or even nature. Since we are a union of body and soul, we use physical objects to help point us to spiritual realities.

Unlike some non-Catholic forms of meditation, we're not seeking to empty our minds or somehow lose our personal identity. Our goal is to enter into conversation and communion with God, to form a relationship with a Person. So instead of trying to empty our minds, we're trying to fill our minds up with God. As Jesus says, "You shall love the Lord your God with all your heart, and with all your soul, and with all your strength, and with all your mind" (Luke 10:27).

Meditation is a non-negotiable in the spiritual life. As St. Teresa of Ávila says, "Without mental prayer a person becomes either a brute or a devil. If you do not practice mental prayer, you do not need any devil to throw you into hell, you throw yourself in there of your own accord."[2] She also says that "Meditation is the basis for acquiring all the virtues, and to undertake it is a matter of life and death for all Christians."[3]

As far as the steps of meditation, the first thing to do is find a good time and quiet place. We have to silence the exterior noise which is always threatening to drown out our interior lives. The saints say that the best time of day for meditation is early in the morning. If you can, go to the same prayer spot on a daily basis. Posture makes a difference, as well. Be comfortable, but make sure to sit upright in a position that's not going to lead your mind to wander.

The second step is recollection. The goal of recollection is to calm all those voices and ideas that are zipping through your mind and place yourself at the feet of Christ. It can be difficult, but don't get discouraged if you have a hard time. St. Teresa of Ávila says, "Do not imagine that the important thing is never to be

---

[2] Chautard, Dom Jean-Baptiste., *The Soul of the Apostolate* Part 3 No. 2

[3] St. Teresa of Ávila., *The Way of Perfection* Ch. 16

thinking of anything else and that if your mind becomes slightly distracted all is lost."[4] So if your mind wanders a bit, don't worry about it.

That said, it's obviously better if we can diminish those distractions and stay in contact with Christ. And there are some practical ways to do this. One effective way to recollect is to simply repeat the name of Jesus over and over until you calm down and focus your attention on him. Another method is to say a very slow Our Father or Hail Mary. Also, ask the Holy Spirit to help you recollect so that you can enter more deeply into prayer.

The third step is the actual meditation using your chosen input. For example, if it's a book like the Bible, first choose a passage (e.g. the Gospels) and begin to read the passage slowly. Don't read it for information. Read it for relationship. As you're reading, a particular verse, phrase, or word might strike you. Pause your reading and ask the Lord about it. "What does this mean, Lord?" "What are you trying to show me?" Let him speak to you in your heart. Ponder on it. When the moment is over or you get distracted, go back to your reading. That's meditation in a nutshell. But don't forget that once the Lord begins to show you things through what you're reading—and most of the time he will—you have to resolve to act on it. That's the last step. Pray for the grace you need and make an act of the will to follow through.

Don't worry if nothing strikes you from your meditation. That may happen and it's totally okay. Just spending time with the Lord is building your relationship with him and he loves it.

With regard to length of time, if you've never tried to practice meditation, start with ten to fifteen minutes. It will be hard, but if you continue to do it the time will eventually pass more quickly because spending time with the Lord in prayer is literally what you're made for.

Lesson Introduction

Two of the most important topics —especially for beginners in the spiritual life— are spiritual consolations and dryness in prayer. That said, many people have mistaken views about what they are, why they occur, and what to do when they happen. But it's crucial to understand them correctly so that you can continue to make spiritual progress no matter what you're experiencing.

In fact, as we explore these seemingly opposite ends of the prayer spectrum, we'll discover that things aren't always what they seem.

---

[4] St. Teresa of Ávila., *Interior Castle*, Fourth Mansion, Ch. 1

🎥 **NOW BEGIN THE VIDEO**

Notes

_____

_____

_____

_____

_____

_____

_____

What the Saints Say

"I call it consolation when an interior movement is aroused in the soul, by which it is inflamed with love of its Creator and Lord, and as a consequence, can love no creature on the face of the earth for its own sake, but only in the Creator of them all.

It is likewise consolation when one sheds tears that move to the love of God, whether it be sorrow for sins, or because of the sufferings of Christ our Lord, or for any other reason that is immediately directed to the praise and service of God.

Finally, I call consolation every increase of faith, hope, and love, and all interior joy that invites and attracts to what is heavenly and to the salvation of one's soul by filling it with peace and quiet in its Creator and Lord."

ST. IGNATIUS OF LOYOLA—*16th Century Founder of the Society of Jesus (Jesuits) & author of the famous* Spiritual Exercises

🔊Play Guided Audio Meditation

"I meditate on all that thou hast done; I muse on what thy hands have wrought. I stretch out my hands to thee; my soul thirsts for thee like a parched land. I stretch out my hands to You; My soul longs for You, as a parched land."

PSALM 143:6

Further Reflection

While spiritual consolations, dryness and even desolations from the Evil One are all ultimately given or permitted by God, there's also a sense in which our very progress in the spiritual life can be the cause of some bittersweet sentiments in our own heart.

This happens when the sweetness of early spiritual consolations is eventually replaced not only with aridity and a lack of feelings, but by a more acute awareness of both the majesty of God and our own abysmal state.

In other words, as we grow in the spiritual life, we more clearly recognize our all-encompassing, all-loving perfect Father for who he is, and even our joys become laced with angst over the myriad of times we've denied our Lord. Like Peter we cry out, "Depart from me, Lord, for I am a sinful man" (Luke 5:8).

And yet at the same time, the increasing knowledge of our own weakness is also the source of our greatest consolation in Jesus Christ. As the Lord declared to St. Paul, "My grace is sufficient for you, for my power is made perfect in weakness" (2 Corinthians 12:9).

As time passes and our understanding increases, the tears we've shed due to our weakness eventually become tears of joy as Christ's power is made all the more perfect in our life. We understand more and more fully that God is always leading us and helping us toward an unspeakably joyful union with him in spite of our sinfulness. He loves us and his mercy always surrounds us. All we have to do is keep seeking, keep trusting, and allow him to draw us ever closer.

Review Questions

1. What are spiritual consolations?

2. What is the danger of spiritual consolations?

3. Why does God allow dryness in prayer?

4. What does St. John of the Cross call the period of dryness leading up to the second stage of the spiritual life—the Illuminative Way? Why?

5. What should you do when you start experiencing dryness in prayer or the "night of sense"?

Discussion Questions

1. Have you ever experienced any spiritual consolations? If so, what were you doing when it happened? If you're comfortable doing so, share what it felt like. Did it happen often?

2. If you have not experienced any spiritual consolations, do you desire them? How does it make you feel knowing that it's not unusual to never receive them?

3. Have you ever felt a period of dryness in prayer? Before watching the video, did you know that it can be a sign of growth and a "good" thing? What did you do when you experienced the dryness? How might you deal with it now having watched this lesson?

4. Having progressed through two-thirds of this study, take a moment and reflect on your current prayer life. Has it changed since you first began this series? If so, how? If not, why? Have you seen real progress? Are there any particular issues or things with which you're struggling?

📖 Further Reading

Catechism of the Catholic Church, paragraph 2731

Prayer Journal

LESSON SEVEN

Contemplation & Communion

What We Covered in Our Last Lesson

Two important issues that often come into play relatively early on in our lives of prayer are spiritual consolations and dryness. Both are powerful tools the Lord uses to help us grow up in the spiritual life.

SPIRITUAL CONSOLATIONS

When a person has a powerful spiritual awakening, they often go all-in on the spiritual life.

As time goes by they begin to understand that a huge part of the early stages is a stripping away of the world. They embrace the underlying idea and goal of a "purgative" way and start to rid themselves of things that keep them from God.

Oftentimes when God sees these "beginners" in the spiritual life really focus and begin to make these sacrifices, he rewards them with what are called spiritual or sensible consolations—little tastes of heaven even as they temper their taste for the things of the world. These spiritual consolations are something you actually feel and most of the time they happen during prayer. They can range from a deep sense of peace to actual sensations of the power of the Holy Spirit, among other things.

That said, many people will never experience spiritual consolations. For whatever reason God decides they don't need them or shouldn't receive them. If you're making progress without them, don't worry if you don't receive any of these consolations.

For those that do, there is a danger of getting caught up in these spiritual consolations and confusing these sensations and feelings for spiritual growth. These consolations are nothing more than a mere foretaste of what is to come and if we focus on them, we'll lose sight of the main goal of God himself.

Remember that spiritual growth isn't about any kind of "euphoria" or how we feel. It's about how we live. Progress is measured by the manifestation of the fruits of the Spirit listed in Galatians 5: "love, joy, peace, patience, kindness, goodness, faithfulness, gentleness, self-control" (vv. 22–23).

DRYNESS IN PRAYER

Aware of the trap into which spiritual consolations can lead us, God knows exactly how to divert our attention away from good feelings and begin to mature us in our relationship with him. This is where dryness in prayer begins to play a role—the opposite end of the spectrum of prayer. As we continue to progress toward him, he begins to disallow us from feeling much of his presence. Whereas before you really felt the nearness of God, now you feel little.

The reason is that he is preparing us to move out of the first stage of the spiritual life—the Purgative Way—and into the second stage—the Illuminative Way. In other words, we've reached a transition stage in which he's teaching us to grow up. He's teaching us to seek him not because of what we feel or what he gives us, but for who he is in himself.

St. John of the Cross calls this transition the "passive purification of the senses"—or the "night" of sense. And he calls it a "night" because our relationship with God has become a bit more obscure, so to speak. But while we don't feel him as much, God hasn't gone anywhere. In fact, he's actually gotten closer to us. We just haven't yet developed the spiritual senses to experience him on this new level.

St. John of the Cross uses the analogy of the sun to describe this. He points out that if you look directly at the sun you're blinded, not because of lack of light, but because you don't have the senses to look right into its incredible luminosity. That's like what's happening in this "night" of sense. As we move into this transition, we don't sense God's presence because we haven't yet developed the spiritual senses to experience him on a deeper level. We don't feel him because we keep trying to find him with our natural senses. We keep looking for that euphoria, peace, or any kind of sensible feeling of his presence. But God is trying to coax us into a deeper relationship that isn't simply based on feelings.

It's kind of like the difference between the butterflies a person feels in early dating and the deep love of a long-married couple that endures all the mountains and valleys of life. God wants a real union with us that isn't subject to the whims of childish feelings. So as long as we are doing what we're supposed to do in the spiritual life—daily prayer, getting to Mass, striving for virtue, dryness isn't a bad thing. It's actually a sign of growth.

In fact, the saints say that when we feel this kind of dryness and still seek the Lord in prayer, it's actually more meritorious than when we are sailing right along in the spiritual life. The reason is because by seeking him when we don't feel like it, we are showing him that we love him no matter what we feel or don't feel.

So when you hit this stage of dryness in prayer, don't worry that you're doing something wrong. Just keep showing up to daily prayer. God is maturing you in the faith. In fact, John of the Cross likens it all to a mother weaning her child. He says, "As the child grows older, the mother withholds her caresses and hides her tender love; she rubs bitter aloes on her sweet breast and sets the child down from her arms, letting it walk on its own feet so that it may put aside the habits of childhood and grow accustomed to greater and more important things."[5]

Lesson Introduction

It's time to turn our attention to the third, and highest form of prayer—contemplation. And what we'll quickly discover is that while each of us is made to receive and engage in this incredible mode of prayer, it can be challenging to discuss. Why? Because it is otherworldly. It is supernatural.

Even so, we need to know what it is and how to prepare ourselves to receive it.

 **NOW BEGIN THE VIDEO**

Notes

---

[5] St. John of the Cross, *Dark Night of the Soul,* Book 1, Section 2

What the Saints Say

"Contemplation is nothing else than a secret, peaceful, and loving infusion of God, which if admitted, will set the soul on fire with the Spirit of love."

ST. JOHN OF THE CROSS—*16th Century Spanish Carmelite & "Mystical Doctor"*

◀ Play Guided Audio Meditation

"O God, thou art my God, I seek thee,

my soul thirsts for thee;

my flesh faints for thee,

as in a dry and weary land where no water is.

So I have looked upon thee in the sanctuary,

beholding thy power and glory.

Because thy steadfast love is better than life,

my lips will praise thee.

So I will bless thee as long as I live;

I will lift up my hands and call on thy name."

PSALM 63:1–4

Further Reflection

When talking about the ins and outs of contemplative prayer it's very easy to forget that at the end of the day, it's all about love. Yes, there are various aspects and details of this very special and incredible type of prayer with which we should become familiar. But we don't want to lose the forest for the trees.

The Christian life is primarily focused upon growing in the love of God and neighbor. It's directed toward a deeper penetration into the eternal exchange of the love of God himself. That's the heart of contemplation. It's a molding and shaping us into the likeness of Jesus.

As St. Paul says, "And we all, with unveiled face, beholding the glory of the Lord, are being changed into his likeness from one degree of glory to another; for this comes from the Lord who is the Spirit" (2 Corinthians 3:18).

In other words, when God grants a person the grace of infused contemplation, he isn't just showing them something. We're not talking about natural vision. We're talking about a kind of divine sight—a contemplation of divine love—that can't help but transform us from the inside out. After all, to see him is to love him. And the more we begin to experience God this way, the more we cry out along with the Psalmist "My soul longs, yea, faints for the courts of the Lord; my heart and flesh sing for joy to the living God" (Psalm 84:2).

Contemplation is the highest mode of prayer because it is the beginning of the end—the beginning of our full immersion into the river of divine love in which we were made to live for all eternity.

Review Questions

1. Why is it so hard to easily describe contemplative prayer?

2. Can we do anything to cause contemplative prayer ourselves?

3. What can we do to prepare ourselves for the gift of contemplation?

4. To what celebration does the *Catechism* directly connect our reception of contemplation?

5. What happens in our prayer life to let us know we're beginning to enter into contemplative prayer?

6. What is the end result of moving into contemplation? What does it do to us?

Discussion Questions

1. Does the concept of contemplative prayer make sense to you? How does your understanding of it differ after watching the lesson? Was there something in particular from the video that struck you or helped you come to a deeper understanding of it? Does contemplation sound like something you desire?

2. Have you ever experienced the nudge of the Holy Spirit to stop doing your regular meditations and simply sit with the Lord? If so, what did you do and what was your experience with it? Are you the kind of person who finds it difficult to not be "doing something" in prayer?

3. In the lesson, Matthew discussed the fact that as you move into contemplation, in addition to experiencing dryness in prayer, you begin to lose your attraction to the things of the world. You may even lose the satisfaction associated with doing good works and apostolic activity. Does this loss of satisfaction scare you at all? Why do you think this happens?

4. At the end of the lesson, Matthew made the point that contemplation isn't something reserved for people whose lives are mostly dedicated to prayer like monks and nuns in mountaintop monasteries. Rather, since we're all designed for deep union with God, contemplative prayer is something for every one of us. If you didn't think this was the case previously, do you still struggle with that idea? Do you fully believe that God wants to give you this great gift when he thinks you're ready? Why?

Further Reading

Chapter 8 of *Prayer Works: Getting a Grip on Catholic Spirituality* by Matthew Leonard

Prayer Journal

LESSON EIGHT

Overcoming Distraction & The Power of Silence

What We Covered in Our Last Lesson

While contemplation is the "high point" of our prayer lives, it's difficult to talk about. That's because it is supernatural. It comes directly from God and only he can make it happen. As the *Catechism of the Catholic Church* says, "it is a gift, a grace; it can be accepted only in humility and poverty" (CCC 2713).

While in vocal prayer and meditation there is a sense that we are the impetus—actively talking, reading, or reflecting—contemplation is all God. In other words, contemplation is less about what we do and more about what God does in us. While vocal prayer and meditation are more about our *activity* in prayer, contemplation is more about our *receptivity*. We can open our spiritual arms, so to speak, but only God can grant the gift of this deeper prayer.

As St. Teresa of Ávila wrote, God grants this intimacy "to whom He wills, when He wills, and as He wills."

Purely speaking, contemplation is what we call an infused prayer. It's a silent filling up of God's presence in the depths of our soul in a movement completely initiated by the Lord. St. John of the Cross describes it as a "secret and peaceful and loving inflow of God."

In this new kind of prayer, something fresh and powerful is happening. God is welling up in us and allowing us to experience the living waters of his presence, the living waters Christ described to the woman at the well in John chapter 4. And we experience this welling up, this deeper, more intense level of communion with God as contemplative prayer.

But what exactly is contemplative prayer? The *Catechism* says, "It is a gaze of faith fixed on Jesus, an attentiveness to the Word of God, a silent love" (CCC 2724). It is a quiet, interior prayer initiated by God where he begins to give us the desire to put our meditations aside and sit quietly with him. It's a prayer in which he wants to commune with us more directly.

To illuminate this deeper kind of communion, the *Catechism* describes a direct connection and similarity between contemplative prayer and the mystical movement of the Mass. Paragraph 2711 says, *"Entering into contemplative prayer is like entering into the Eucharistic liturgy: we 'gather up' the heart, recollect our whole being under the prompting of the Holy Spirit, abide in the dwelling place of the Lord which we are, awaken our faith in order to enter into the presence of him who awaits us."*

A few paragraphs later in 2718, it says, "The mystery of Christ is celebrated by the Church in the Eucharist, and the Holy Spirit makes it come alive in contemplative prayer." So contemplative prayer is us being drawn into God in a way that complements, parallels, and intensifies what happens when we receive the Eucharist.

Even so, just because it's a more intense movement of God doesn't necessarily mean we'll detect it with our senses. We're talking about a direct encounter in the soul. St. John of the Cross says, "At this time, God does not communicate himself through the senses as he did before…, but begins to communicate himself through pure spirit by an act of simple contemplation in which there is no discursive succession of thought."[6]

Practically speaking, when moving into contemplation you begin to lose your ability to meditate as you did previously. It becomes hard. You experience a kind of dryness in prayer (and perhaps even a lack of satisfaction in apostolic activity). None of this means you desire God less. Rather, you feel a desire to set aside your meditative material and now simply want to "be" with God, to sit quietly in his presence in a gaze of silent love. As the peasant told the Curé of Ars, "I look at him and he looks at me" (CCC 2715).

With regard to how long it takes, generally speaking the move into contemplative prayer takes a while. Exactly how long differs from person to person. In terms of the three stages of the spiritual life we discussed earlier, the early movements of infused contemplation begin in the latter part of the first stage, the Purgative Way. This makes sense because part of what's happening is that God is "purging" us of our need to experience him through feelings or emotions.

The point of the diminishing sense of his presence and lack of satisfaction in good works isn't because he wants to diminish our happiness. Rather, he's preparing us for a more intense and enduring happiness with him in eternity. To do that, he's shifting our focus to him directly, instead of having us focus on things related to him.

Finally, we have to realize that while some people think contemplative prayer is only reserved for monks, nuns, and "super holy" people, it's actually a level of prayer for which each of us is designed. It's for everyone, regardless of your state in life. Our job to prepare for this union is receive the sacraments regularly, keep

---

[6] St. John of the Cross, *Dark Night of the Soul*, Bk 1, Ch 9

our times of prayer consistently, and make the effort to live the gospel faithfully. This paves the way, so to speak, for God to grant the gift of contemplative prayer at his discretion.

Lesson Introduction

One of the essential elements of the life of recollection and prayer is silence. It plays a massive role in the spiritual life. Unfortunately, it's not so easy to come by. In fact, interior recollection is difficult even when everything "outside" is quiet. But we have to cultivate quiet in our lives if we're going to really pray.

In this lesson we'll talk about how to attain interior silence, as well as how to deal with one of the most dangerous pitfalls to our silence into which we can fall. Namely, incorrect use of the tongue.

 **NOW BEGIN THE VIDEO**

Notes

What the Saints Say

"Wisdom enters through love, silence, and mortification. It is great wisdom to know how to be silent and to look at neither the remarks, nor the deeds, nor the lives of others."

ST. JOHN OF THE CROSS—*16th Century Spanish Carmelite & Mystical Doctor*

◀ Play Guided Audio Meditation

"And there he came to a cave, and lodged there; and behold, the word of the Lord came to him, and he said to him, 'What are you doing here, Eli'jah?'

He said, 'I have been very jealous for the Lord, the God of hosts; for the people of Israel have forsaken thy covenant, thrown down thy altars, and slain thy prophets with the sword; and I, even I only, am left; and they seek my life, to take it away.'

And he said, 'Go forth, and stand upon the mount before the Lord.' And behold, the Lord passed by, and a great and strong wind rent the mountains, and broke in pieces the rocks before the Lord, but the Lord was not in the wind; and after the wind an earthquake, but the Lord was not in the earthquake; and after the earthquake a fire, but the Lord was not in the fire; and after the fire a still small voice.

And when Eli'jah heard it, he wrapped his face in his mantle and went out and stood at the entrance of the cave."

1 KINGS 19:9–13

Further Reflection

"The tongue is a fire..." (James 3:6).

That about says it all. St. James is warning us that if we use our tongue to denigrate and destroy others or speak against God, we participate in the hate of the Evil One who burns in the fires of hell. It's pretty serious stuff.

James, and other biblical writers, speak so forcefully about the tongue because they are fully aware of its immense power. Even though comparatively small, it greatly controls our movement up or down the spiritual mountain. "Look at the ships also," says James, "though they are so great and are driven by strong winds, they are guided by a very small rudder wherever the will of the pilot directs. So the tongue is a little member and boasts of great things. How great a forest is set ablaze by a small fire" (3:4–5)!

It is imperative that we control the tongue. And one of the most effective ways to do it is to control all the things we allow into our head and heart. Fill them with garbage and that's what will come out. Fill them with God, and good speech will follow, "for out of the abundance of [the] heart the mouth speaks" (Luke 6:45).

Speech is obviously necessary, but it needs to purified. Pray for the grace to mortify the sinful pleasure that comes from derogatory speech and seek to build up the Body of Christ through loving words. As St. Paul says, "Let no evil talk come out of your mouths, but only such as is good for edifying, as fits the occasion, that it may impart grace to those who hear" (Ephesians 4:29).

Review Questions

1. What are the two types of distractions and how do they differ?

2. How can involuntary distractions actually help us?

3. Why are voluntary distractions venial sin?

4. What's the main reason we need to cultivate silence in order to grow in the spiritual life?

5. Why doesn't the Devil want us to cultivate silence?

6. What are some practical ways we can cultivate more silence and "constant prayer" in our lives?

Discussion Questions

1. How do you usually deal with distractions when they arise in prayer? What have you learned from what we've discussed in this lesson that will help you in the future?

2. In thinking about your time of prayer, have you noticed one or two major themes that dominate your involuntary distractions? In other words, are there certain things that pop into your head on a regular basis when you try to focus? How might you go about letting go of these distractions?

3. Understanding the nature of voluntary distractions and the fact that they are venial sin can be surprising, to say the least. Many people have never been taught about them. Having heard this lesson, are there things in your life that may fall into the category of voluntary distraction? If so, what practical steps can you take to deal with them so you can focus more upon the Lord?

4. Have you ever had an interior longing for more silence? It can be hard, especially depending upon family life and work schedules, but do you have a certain time of the day when you try to "get away" and find some peace and quiet even for a few moments? If you could cut out more of the "noise" in your life, what would it be?

Had you ever considered that, in a way, your desire for silence is a desire for God? How does that idea strike you? Does it change the way you understand the role of silence in the spiritual life?

Further Reading

Chapter 9 of *Prayer Works: Getting a Grip on Catholic Spirituality* by Matthew Leonard

Prayer Journal

LESSON NINE

Making Real Progress

What We Covered in Our Last Lesson

In order to prepare ourselves for contemplative prayer, we need to learn how to fight against distractions and understand the powerful role of silence.

The *Catechism* says that "The habitual difficulty in prayer is *distraction*. It can affect words and their meaning in vocal prayer; it can concern, more profoundly, Him to whom we are praying, in vocal prayer,... meditation, and contemplative prayer" (CCC 2729).

There are two types of distraction: voluntary and involuntary. Involuntary distractions are thoughts that come into your head while you're trying to focus. They happen to everyone and are not a big deal. St. Teresa of Ávila says we should let these wanderings of our mind come and go. In fact, she says they can actually be turned into a prayer if we offer them back to the Lord as soon as we realize we're being distracted.

Involuntary distraction can actually become a powerful ally in prayer. The *Catechism* says that "a distraction reveals to us what we are attached to" (CCC 2729). In other words, they show us the things in our life with which we are most preoccupied. They show us the things we need to deal with, or that we need to let go of.

Voluntary distractions, on the other hand, are those which we allow to hang around when they pop up, or only half-heartedly attempt to squash when they come bouncing along.

When we entertain *involuntary* distractions that come along—make an act of the will and let them hang around—they move from the category of involuntary to voluntary.

But sometimes it's not just the distracting thought itself that's a problem. Sometimes we're voluntarily creating the distraction in the first place. For example, if you can't effectively enter into prayer because you can't get a television show you've been bingeing on out of your head—and you continue to watch it—you've created a voluntary distraction. In other words, you're causing the distraction. Even though you know it's causing issues in prayer, you're making an act of the will to keep bingeing on the show.

Voluntary distraction is actually venial sin. Why? Because by voluntarily allowing distractions to keep us from engaging God, we are deliberately choosing something else over God. Don't forget that prayer is an audience God lovingly grants us. By continuing to choose a distraction of our own creation, we're basically telling God he isn't as important as that distraction. So we need to take action to turn away from these once we recognize them. The beautiful thing is that once we take that action, those voluntary distractions have now become *involuntary* and we can just offer them right back to God.

(If you deal with scrupulosity, please seek advice from a priest, counselor, or someone else you trust on this topic so that you don't mistakenly reject good and normal things as distractions.)

SILENCE

Related to this whole idea of distractions is the topic of silence. If we're not silent in body and spirit, we can't hear God. As St. John of the Cross says, "The Father spoke one Word, which was his Son, and this Word he speaks always in eternal silence, and in silence must it be heard by the soul."[7]

While noise and activity are a natural part of life, we have to cultivate other, more silent parts of life, as well, if we're going to grow in relationship with God. This is because we are ultimately made for the beautiful silence of God. In himself—in his inner life—God is silent. That's one of the reasons why as we progress from vocal prayer to meditation to contemplation, it all becomes more silent. We're entering into the silent, loving dialogue of the Trinity. As paragraph 2717 of the *Catechism* says, "Contemplative prayer is *silence*, the 'symbol of the world to come.'"

Yes, we'll make a joyful noise unto the Lord in heaven, but there's also a real sense in which we encounter God most deeply in the depths of his silent love. Both Jesus and many saints throughout the millennia make it clear that we can't enter into a true relationship with God unless we cultivate silence.

Of course, it seems like the world is doing everything it can to keep us from attaining to this silent love of God. Society feels the need for constant diversion and noise because there's a sense in which silence is scary. It forces us to be alone with ourselves and take a look in the mirror. And the Evil One doesn't want us seeking any kind of deeper meaning in life.

But the Devil also hates silence because in its essence silence is sacred. Why? Because it's connected with God. That's why we naturally turn to silence when we encounter the Lord, like in a beautiful church. And this relationship between silence and the presence of God plays out very powerfully in our lives of prayer. The more we climb the prayer ladder through meditation and contemplation,

---

[7] St. John of the Cross, *Sayings of Light and Love*, 100

the more silent our conversation with God becomes. As St. Augustine said, "To the extent that the Word—the Word made man—grows in us, words diminish."

Given its importance, we need to ask ourselves how we can cultivate silence. As discussed in a previous lesson, when trying to become recollected so as to actively pray, we can slowly say the Our Father or prayerfully repeat the name of Jesus.

But what about the rest of the day when not actively praying? The first thing to do is examine what we're putting into our mind since all of it becomes food for the imagination. It's also important to look at *when* we're consuming things. We need time to become silent. We can't just snap our fingers and suddenly become quiet interiorly. Put simply, we need to begin making decisions based around how things will affect our ability to be silent with God.

While this may sound difficult, remember that we are not doing this on our own. God is doing it to us. Yes, we have to make an act of the will and decide to seek him. But the closer we get to him, the more his desires become our desires. The things that attracted us so powerfully before, lose their luster in the light of Christ. As time goes by, we begin to want silence because we know that's where we encounter the Lord.

Lesson Introduction

In order to make progress in the life of prayer and climb the spiritual ladder, there are three powerful keys: perseverance, humility, and confidence.

And while they're supremely important, we also have to realize that our spiritual life needs to fully adapt to our state in life. If it doesn't, we can harm both our own progress, as well as that of others.

 **NOW BEGIN THE VIDEO**

Notes

What the Saints Say

"The most powerful weapon to conquer the devil is humility. For, as he does not know at all how to employ it, neither does he know how to defend himself from it."

SAINT VINCENT DE PAUL—*17th Century French Priest & Founder of the Daughters of Charity*

◀ Play Guided Audio Meditation

"With what shall I come before the Lord,

and bow myself before God on high?

Shall I come before him with burnt offerings,

with calves a year old?

Will the Lord be pleased with thousands of rams,

with ten thousands of rivers of oil?

Shall I give my first-born for my transgression,

the fruit of my body for the sin of my soul?"

He has showed you, O man, what is good;

and what does the Lord require of you

but to do justice, and to love kindness,

and to walk humbly with your God?"

MICAH 6:6–8

Further Reflection

Just as pride has "pride of place" amongst the capital sins, humility reigns in the life of virtue. It's a massive key to the spiritual life. In her famous work *Interior Castle,* St. Teresa of Ávila sums it up by stating that "without humility all will be lost."

Ever the deadly enemy, pride crushes our prayer life because it places limits on what God can do in our life. It seeks our own glory and subordinates the Lord, placing him below his own creatures. We can't allow that to happen.

The great spiritual writer Fr. Eugene Boylan declared that "God cannot pour out His gifts to the proud without self-contradiction as long as they are obstinate in their attitude."[8] In other words, pride is the total opposite of God, and our relationship with him—our life of prayer—is totally dependent upon the virtue of humility. By its very nature, authentic prayer requires we place ourselves not above, but at the feet of our Lord. We are always to be children crying out to our Father in heaven.

And to that end, we must always be examining ourselves, assessing the content of our hearts. Are we seeking ourselves in prayer or God? "Lord, may we always seek you above all else."

Review Questions

1. Why do we need perseverance in order to make progress in prayer and the spiritual life?

2. Why is the virtue of humility so key to the life of prayer?

3. What parable did Christ use to teach about the necessity of humility?

4. According to Fr. Nicholas Grou, what act of God proves the dignity and value of our soul in his eyes and should fill us with confidence?

---

[8] Boylan, Fr. Eugene, *This Tremendous Lover*, Ch. 7

5. How does a person's vocation or state in life affect their prayer life?

Discussion Questions

1. Think about your daily life of prayer. Would you say you are able to mostly persevere when encountering difficulties in prayer? Can you think of an example of when you did or didn't? Have you ever directly asked God for the grace of perseverance? If not, would you now consider it important?

2. Certainly praying for humility can be difficult. Have you ever done it? What happened? Were you surprised by what the Lord did? If you haven't, what keeps you from doing so?

3. Is it hard for you to have confidence that God will hear and answer your prayers? If not, why do you think that's the case? Can you think of some times when God obviously answered your prayers? What are some occasions when he answered in a totally unexpected way? What are some passages or stories in Scripture you can meditate upon that might help you gain more confidence?

4. As discussed in the lesson, different vocations are going to have different rhythms of prayer and different spiritual lives in general. The mother of small children is going to find it far more difficult to carve out time with God than a cloistered nun. Have you ever tried to do too much in the spiritual life and neglected your duties based on your state in life? How? On the flip side of the coin, have you ever used your state in life as an excuse not to pray? If so, what was the situation?

5. Sometimes it feels like we're barely hanging on given the warp speed of life. Have you ever felt guilty that you're not doing more spiritually because you're going so many different directions? If so, is that something you've taken to prayer?

With your particular vocation in mind, are there perhaps some things you can change that might help you appropriately structure your prayer life while still fulfilling the duties of your station in life?

Further Reading

Chapters 10–12 of *Prayer Works: Getting a Grip on Catholic Spirituality* by Matthew Leonard

Prayer Journal

What We Covered In Our Last Lesson

There are three fundamental things we can focus upon that will help us make real progress in prayer and the spiritual life in general: perseverance, humility, and confidence.

PERSEVERANCE

Perhaps the most vital quality we need to have is perseverance. Deciding to have a real life of prayer is a daily act of the will where we have to fight against our human weaknesses. As the *Catechism* says, "prayer is a battle" (CCC 2725). There are going to be a lot of days when we simply don't feel like it. We have to fight against those feelings and persist in seeking the Lord.

The parable of the persistent friend teaches us that untiringly asking God for good things places us in the correct position of a child in relation to the Father. By teaching us persistence, he's helping us realize that ultimately, every good thing comes from him.

HUMILITY

Humility comes from the Latin word "*humus,*" which means earth, soil, or ground. It is a bowing down to the ground before God in recognition of who we are in relation to him. It means recognizing the reality of our smallness, our utter inferiority.

Humility is an absolute necessity because it's the virtue that crushes the most powerful of all the deadly sins—pride. It was pride that led Adam to commit the first sin back in the Garden of Eden. It is the humble obedience of the New Adam, Jesus Christ, that saves us. Put simply, humility is necessary for progress because it makes us like Christ, which is the ultimate goal.

St. John Chrysostom says that the combination of humility and sin is better than a mixture of virtue and pride. To illustrate his point, he references the parable of the publican and the Pharisee in Luke 18. In his pride, the Pharisee thinks he deserves God's positive response to his prayer because of what he does for God. But the publican stands in back to offer his prayer because he knows he's not worthy of God. Like the publican, we need to throw ourselves into the arms of God, beat our breasts, and beg for his mercy.

If we do that, we can be assured that God will hear us and help us.

CONFIDENCE

Confidence flows from humility because we're not appealing to God based on our own goodness or merits. We're humbly appealing to the goodness of God himself and the merits of Jesus Christ.

Many people have an issue with confidence. They don't feel worthy and have a hard time grasping the fact that God will take care of them because they've been mistreated or wounded by others. But God will never let us down. He is a perfect Father who loves us more than we can possibly imagine. He longs for us and wants to be in a deep, loving relationship with us.

Don't forget that the Lord gave himself up for us—literally died for us—so that we would have the opportunity to move into a real relationship of loving communion with the Most Holy Trinity. That's why we can have confidence. Ultimately, our movement into relationship with him isn't dependent upon our strengths and weaknesses. It is dependent upon his all-powerful love which saves us.

STATE IN LIFE

Our spiritual lives are supposed to correspond to our state in life – our vocation. A father or mother's spiritual life is going to look very different from that of a Bishop, priest, or hermit. Each has duties and responsibilities that are required by their particular station in life.

The flip side is that we can't use our duties in life as an excuse to not be serious about our prayers and interior life. It's always a both/and. That said, finding the proper balance between the interior and exterior life, between prayer and the life of service to others, can be difficult. In fact, there may be times when you can't pray at all because of some unexpected event or emergency. When that happens, snatch the times of prayer you can manage. Having a reasonable level of flexibility in our spiritual life is important. Jesus himself demonstrated this when he ministered to the crowds when all he wanted to do was mourn the death of John the Baptist.

That kind of self-giving love is exactly what the life of prayer is trying to help you do. So take care of what needs to be taken care of as situations present themselves. That said, be careful. Flexibility is one thing. Regularly canceling your normal time to be alone with God is another. We can't use other issues as a consistent excuse for not spending time with the Lord.

Finally, never lose sight of the deep joy that results from a life of relationship with Christ. It is far beyond anything else this world can offer and is literally the life for which you are designed. And that life—that relationship—only happens through a real life of prayer.

Please, let this study be a springboard into a life-changing relationship with the God who loves you like no other. A regular life of prayer is your pathway into a purposeful, happy life on earth and a mind-blowing, ecstatic union with him for all eternity.

APPENDIX

COMMON CATHOLIC PRAYERS

Our Father

Our Father, Who art in heaven,

Hallowed be Thy name.

Thy kingdom come.

Thy will be done, on earth as it is in heaven.

Give us this day our daily bread.

And forgive us our trespasses,

as we forgive those who trespass against us.

And lead us not into temptation,

but deliver us from evil.

Amen.

Come Holy Spirit

Come, Holy Spirit, fill the hearts of thy faithful and enkindle in them the fire of thy love.

V. Send forth thy Spirit and they shall be created.

R. And thou shalt renew the face of the earth.

Let us pray. O God, who didst instruct the hearts of the faithful by the light of the Holy Spirit, grant

us the same Spirit to be truly wise, and ever rejoice in his consolation. Through Christ our Lord.

Amen.

Hail Mary

Hail Mary, Full of Grace, The Lord is with thee. Blessed art thou among women, and blessed is the fruit of thy womb, Jesus. Holy Mary, Mother of God, pray for us sinners now, and at the hour of our death.

Amen.

Glory Be

Glory be to the Father,

and to the Son,

and to the Holy Spirit.

As it was in the beginning, is now,

and ever shall be; world without end.

Amen

Anima Christi (Soul of Christ)

Soul of Christ, sanctify me.

Body of Christ, save me.

Blood of Christ, inebriate me.

Water from the side of Christ, wash me.

Passion of Christ, strengthen me.

O good Jesus, hear me.

Within Thy Wounds hide me.

Suffer me not to be separated from Thee.

From the malignant enemy, defend me.

In the hour of my death, call me,

And bid me to come to Thee.

That with Thy saints, I may praise Thee.

Forever and ever.

Amen.

Prayer to St. Michael the Archangel

St. Michael the Archangel, defend us in battle

Be our defense against the wickedness and snares of the Devil. May God rebuke him, we humbly pray, and do thou, O Prince of the heavenly hosts, by the power of God, thrust into hell Satan, and all the evil spirits, who prowl about the world seeking the ruin of souls. Amen.

Take the next step!

Experience the entire Science of Sainthood at a huge discount!

"Blown away"

"I can hardly believe how wonderful this is."

Step by step spiritual courses in the Science of Sainthood include:

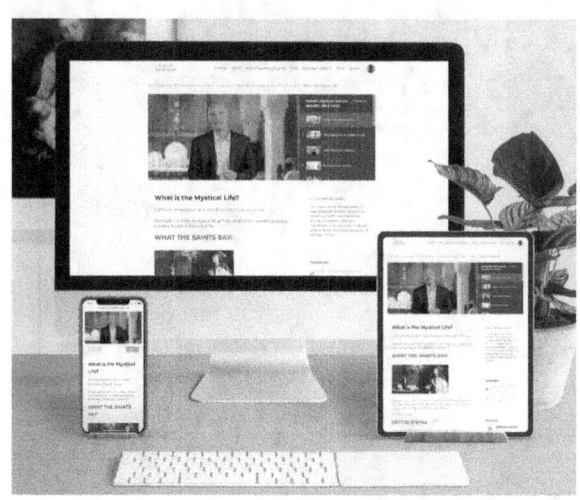

Introduction to Real Prayer

The 7 Deadly Sins

The Moral Virtues

The Theological Virtues

The Dark Night of the Soul

Total Abandonment to God's Will

St. Teresa of Avila's 9 Grades of Prayer

The Gifts of the Spirt *...and a LOT more!*

"If you've ever wanted to deepen your life of prayer and actually make some progress in avoiding vice and growing in virtue, then look no further. The Science of Sainthood is for you."

–**Dr. Brant Pitre**, *Renowned theologian & author of* Jesus and the Jewish Roots of the Eucharist

ScienceofSainthood.com

Scan the QR Code with your Phone's Camera & Tap the Link!

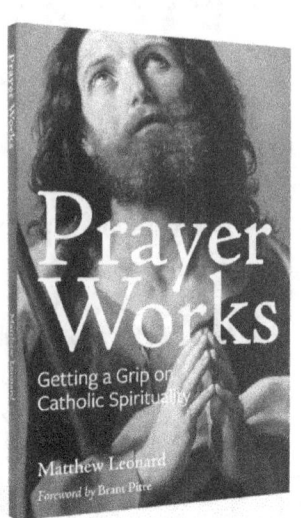

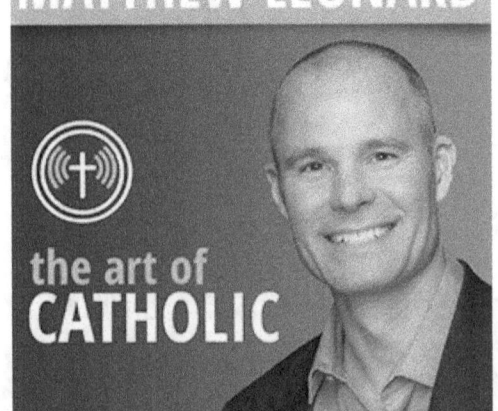